The Handbook
For Helping Kids With
Anxiety And Stress

Featuring Tips For Grown-ups Who Work With Kids,

34 Practical Strategies & Activities

For The Kids Themselves

Kim "Tip" Frank, Ed.S., LPC

Edited by Susan Bowman and Louise Frank.
Layout and design by Tonya Daugherty.

ISBN—1889636576

Library of Congress Number
2003103365

10 9 8 7 6 5 4
Printed in the United States

PO Box 115 • Chapin, SC 29036
(800) 209-9774 • (803) 345-1070 • Fax (803) 345-0888
yl@youthlightbooks.com • www.youthlightbooks.com

Dedication

I am thankful to many people who helped make this book possible.

Thanks to Bob and Susan Bowman

who have always challenged and stretched me to reach my potential.

Thanks to my friends and colleagues, Pat Maness and Sarah Lynn Hayes,

who have given me much encouragement and freedom to grow professionally.

Thanks to my daughter, Rachel,

whose quiet but steady way is an inspiration.

Thanks to my son, Ryan,

whose zeal for life is contagious.

Thanks to my wife, Louise,

for her editing skills and more importantly for being my best friend.

And most of all, I give thanks to God

for making everything possible.

Table Of Contents

Introduction

This book is written in the hopes that children reading this book will find practical help in coping with stress in today's world. People in general, including kids, are stressed more than ever. Everyone experiences stress and fears, which is normal. What is not normal is how stress and fears get in the way of normal living. Simply put, having lasting stress and fears that interfere with normal functioning is called an anxiety disorder. Anxiety disorders ranging in at least six forms afflict 19 million Americans. In January 2002 researchers at UCLA found that less than 25% of Americans with anxiety disorders receive any kind of treatment for their condition (Gorman, 2002). It is my hope that at least in some way more people who are experiencing anxiety in their lives will benefit from the intended practical nature of this book. Through understanding anxiety and finding practical coping strategies, children can gain a greater sense of control in their lives. Happy reading!

Kim "Tip" Frank, Ed.S., LPC

How To Use This Book

This book has two special parts. Part one is mainly written for grown-ups. This section is for parents and professional helpers who are trying to encourage and help children through the trials of anxiety and great stress. Specific tips are provided in this section that help grown-ups set a healing environment for kids. Practical ideas that can be taught to kids are given as well. In addition, a real understanding of anxiety and stress is brought out along with resources that can be tapped to overcome these problems.

Part two is mainly for kids. The strategies shared are for kids young and old. Please note the suggested grade levels given with each strategy. Many of the strategies are out of the ordinary but have proven to work for many children and teenagers. With regular practice, these strategies and techniques can become automatic anxiety and stress relievers. Also included are tips for facing sixteen common fears such as separation anxiety, school phobia, fear of the dark, terrorism, etc. As a backdrop to these coping strategies, a clear explanation is given of what anxiety and stress are and how they affect us. Armed with a good understanding of anxiety and stress along with practical coping strategies, life can and will improve.

Section 1
For Grown-Ups

(but kids are allowed to read, too!)

Does Your Child Have Problems With Anxiety Or Stress?

Anxiety disorders are the most common psychiatric disorders affecting children. According to the National Institute of Mental Health (NIMH), more than 13 percent of children and adolescents during any given six-month period are affected by anxiety disorders (NIMH, 2001). While this is the number one disorder affecting children and teens, it is often unrecognized and untreated.

The picture is not any brighter for adults. According to the most recent data, at least 1 in 4 or 25% of adults will have an anxiety disorder during their lives (Goldman, 2001). If you are facing ongoing stress and anxiety, you are in good company. The good news is that this problem can be helped. Read on!

The following is a checklist of common characteristics of anxiety disorders. How many do you see in your child or teenager?

- Intense fear or discomfort with symptoms such as pounding heart, sweating, trembling, choking, chest pain, nausea, or dizziness.

- Strong fear of dying, losing control, or going crazy.

- Fear of being in places or situations from which escape may be difficult or embarrassing.

- Fear of being outside of home alone; being in a crowd; being on a bridge; traveling on a bus, train or automobile.

- Marked and persistent fear that is excessive or unreasonable cued by the anticipation or presence of a specific object or situation such as airplanes, elevators, heights, storms, water, animals, receiving an injection, seeing blood, loud noises, or costumed characters.

- A marked and persistent fear of one or more social or performance situations in which the child or teen is exposed to unfamiliar peers or to possible scrutiny by others.

- Anxiety that is expressed by crying, tantrums, freezing, or shrinking from social situations with unfamiliar people.

- Recurrent and persistent thoughts, impulses, or images that cause marked anxiety or distress.

- Repetitive behaviors (hand washing, ordering, checking) or mental acts (praying, counting, repeating words silently) that are time consuming and interfere with a person's normal routine.

- Feelings of intense fear, helplessness, or horror after one has experienced an event that involved actual or threatened death or serious injury of self or others.

- Disorganized or agitated behavior after a traumatic event.

- Recurrent and intrusive distressing recollections of a traumatic event or repetitive play or reenactments of traumatic events.

• Behaviors such as difficulty falling or staying asleep, difficulty concentrating, or hyper vigilance.

• Long-lasting, excessive anxiety and worry.

• Anxiety and worry associated with symptoms such as restlessness (feeling keyed up or on edge), being easily fatigued, difficulty concentrating or mind going blank, irritability, muscle tension, and sleep disturbance.

• Anxiety, worry, or physical symptoms that cause distress or impairment in normal functioning in life.

This checklist is adapted from information found in the *Diagnostic and Statistical Manual of Mental Disorders (DSM IV)* (1994, pp. 393-444).

A good rule of thumb is that if you checked more than three or four boxes, it would be wise to speak with a physician and/or mental health professional about your situation. It is always best to rule in or out a problem and enlist good help if needed.

What Exactly Are Anxiety and Stress?

Anxiety as defined by the *DSM IV* is as follows: "The apprehensive anticipation of future danger or misfortune accompanied by a feeling of dysphoria or somatic symptoms of tension. The focus of anticipated danger may be internal or external" *(DSM IV,* 1994, p. 764). In other words, anxiety is worry or fear about things that may happen. Along with this worry or fear are physiological effects such as muscle tension, sweating, rapid heartbeat or restlessness. When anxiety is long lasting and gets in the way of normal functioning, this is then called an anxiety disorder. Several common examples of anxiety disorders are discussed in this book.

Stress is an outgrowth of anxiety. Stress can also grow out of feelings such as anger or guilt among others. Simply put stress is a physical or emotional strain upon the body and mind. Hence stress can be both mental and physical. Strain and pressure equal stress. When the strain or pressure grows too strong, this is then called distress or negative stress. So when a kid is experiencing great anxiety about a test or flying on a plane, this puts a heavy load on the mind and body. See pages 22-23 for examples of the effects of stress on kids.

Common Anxiety Disorders In Kids

The following descriptions of common anxiety disorders found in kids are intended to be only a quick overview of each. To get more in-depth information, the book *Anxiety Disorders in Children and Adolescents: Research, Assessments, and Intervention* by Wendy Silverman and Philip Treffers is an excellent choice. Also note the websites found on page 28.

These six anxiety disorders are common in people young and old. The following information shows us how anxiety disorders come in different forms. As one categorizes various anxiety disorders, specific types of treatments can be developed. In other words, it is important to identify the type of anxiety disorder and treat it accordingly. This is not a complete list, merely the most common. The *Diagnostic and Statistical Manual of Mental Disorders (4th ed.) (DSM IV)* published by the American Psychiatric Association has an extensive listing of anxiety disorders.

Panic Disorder involves severe and frightening periods of strong fears and feelings of doom. An episode may last from a few minutes to several hours. A panic attack may cause chest pains, rapid heartbeat, difficulty breathing, and fear of losing control or dying.

Phobias are a strong fear of a specific object or situation. Fear of animals, insects, storms, seeing blood or receiving an injection, bridges, elevators, heights, and flying are just a few.

Separation Anxiety Disorder involves great worry and stress concerning separation from the home or from those to whom a person is attached. Common fears may include that an accident or illness will happen to a loved one or that he or she will get lost and not get back with loved ones. Refusing to go to school or sleep alone are common characteristics.

Obsessive-Compulsive Disorder (OCD) entails constant thinking (obsessions) about specific things such as germs, doing something wrong or bad, needing to put things in a certain order, or other worries that one cannot put aside. Compulsions involve doing something over and over such as hand washing, ordering, double checking, counting, or repeating words silently. The goal of these compulsions is to stop or lower stress and anxiety.

Post-Traumatic Stress Disorder (PTSD) involves repeated replaying in the mind of a horrifying event over a long period of time. The person experiencing PTSD may have repeated dreams or flashbacks about what happened. During these flashbacks or dreams, he or she may feel as if it was really happening again. He or she may experience jumpiness, difficulty sleeping, and not wanting to go and do normal things. Sometimes, PTSD will not occur until months after a scary or upsetting event.

Generalized Anxiety Disorder involves more than normal worry or anxiety that occurs day after day and month after month. The person finds it difficult to control the tendency to worry. Symptoms include restlessness and feeling keyed up or on edge, often being tired, difficulty concentrating, being moody or irritable, tense muscles, and trouble sleeping.

Good News

Anxiety disorders are the most common type of psychological disorder. That's the bad news. The good news is that anxiety disorders are very treatable. There are many ways to relieve stress and anxiety. The key is to find the ways that work for the person with chronic or intense anxiety and to put them to good use. Here are several approaches that have proven successful for many.

Behavioral Therapy

The key to this approach is facing fears. Little by little the child or teenager is encouraged to face the feared object, event, or situation. As he/she is exposed to his/her fear, the child becomes more comfortable with it. The key is to do this process gradually. Behavioral therapy is considered by many to be the most effective type of therapy for facing specific fears.

Behavioral therapy is a relearning process. Adaptive or helpful behavior is reinforced while maladaptive or unhelpful behaviors are eliminated. Negative behaviors are unlearned and new positive behaviors are learned in their place. One such approach is systematic desensitization where children learn to face and gradually overcome their fears.

Cognitive Therapy

With this type of counseling, children and teenagers are taught to think more positively and constructively. First the child or teenager is taught to recognize negative thought patterns and change them. For example, instead of saying, "I just know it is going to be awful," one might say, "It's tough, but I'll hang in there." How a person thinks about a situation is often more significant than the event itself.

The key to this approach is what one believes about an event or situation. Coping statements are designed to replace self-defeating statements that in turn reduce anxiety. Cognitive therapy can be simply summarized by the following A, B, C's:

A activating event: Thunderstorm		
	B beliefs:	**C** consequences:
irrational	"We're going to get killed"	Intense fear and panic
rational	"I'll just move to a safe spot in the house, and it will be O.K."	Concern about the storm, but calm

Family Therapy

Involving family members in therapy is critical. Family members represent the first line in the support system. As family members work on making things go smoothly in the family, the home becomes a safe haven and a positive source of encouragement. Once family members understand the nature of anxiety disorders, they can encourage the person with an anxiety disorder to stretch himself/herself toward goals set in therapy.

Family therapy intentionally involves the whole family and is based on improving communication and problem solving. Family members can either enable a problem such as anxiety or can set an environment to help the one with the anxiety disorder overcome it. Family members are encouraged to openly communicate and help in the process of solving problems such as intense anxiety that one may be experiencing.

Person-Centered Counseling

Good old catharsis helps virtually everyone. Just talking out a problem can be very valuable. In this approach, the counselor or therapist mainly listens. In addition to listening, facilitative responses such as reflecting feelings, summarizing and clarifying, and asking open questions are used. By using this approach, the client is able to get a clear picture of the problem and figure out ways to effectively deal with it.

The child or teen facing strong anxiety certainly can improve his or her situation by talking through it. Honest expression of feelings and problems is usually the first step in changing a situation for the better. Empathetic responses by a counselor or therapist help immensely, too.

Play Therapy

One of the most effective ways for kids to work out issues is through play. Children express feelings through various play media such as art, puppets, drama, clay, a sand tray, and various toys. Garry Landreth, a leading play therapist, once said, "Toys are the words of the child. Play is the language of the child" (personal communication, July 1992).

This approach is especiallyhelpful to kids who are not very verbal. With the help of a trained play therapist, kids can express many feelings and work out problems through play. Play therapy provides a "kid friendly" environment where children can heal from anxiety and other problems.

Eclectic Counseling Approach

Most effective counseling and therapy involves tailoring the approach to what the child or teen needs. All of the counseling approaches have their merits. Oftentimes it is wise to blend all of these approaches. The kind, empathetic, person-centered approach is always a good place to start. Cognitive and behavioral approaches work hand in hand to confront and overcome anxiety. Enlisting the family's support through family therapy is essential for setting up the child or teen for success. An eclectic approach covers all the bases. For those interested in more in-depth descriptions of types of therapies, please note the following book: *Anxiety Disorders in Children and Adolescents* by John S. March. Also, the websites on page 28 describe approaches to psychotherapy.

Lifestyle Changes

Stopping negative habits such as taking in too much sugar and caffeine is wise. Staying away from alcohol, nicotine, and any recreational drug use is also smart. Make sure you get enough sleep, eat right and allow some free time to have fun. Reading good books helps, too.

What, if any, bad habits does your child have? Have your child list them and purpose to change them. A partner or friend can hold him or her accountable. On the other hand, have your child list two or three good habits he or she would like to develop. Again, an accountability partner can help.

Stop Behaviors

1. _____

2. _____

3. _____

Start Behaviors

1. _____

2. _____

3. _____

Exercise

A good workout or a brisk run or walk can take the edge off of anxiety. When done on a regular basis, the child or teenager will benefit not only physically but also emotionally. Working out continuously for 20 to 30 minutes will help bring balance to a stressed brain. The key is to find an activity your child or teen enjoys. Even if your child is not athletic, just finding an activity that gets the blood pumping is important. The physical and emotional parts of us work together. Strongly encourage your child or teen to get on a regular exercise program. You, as parents, may want to join in.

List one or two exercises your child or teen would enjoy.

Favorite Aerobic Activities

1. _____

2. _____

Alternative Treatments

Learning and practicing relaxation techniques such as breathing exercises and muscle tensing and relaxing are often helpful. Among other possibilities are guided imagery, tapes, meditation, and aromatherapy.

Page 48 of this book called *R and R* lists four such examples of alternative treatments. *The Chill Out Plan* on page 52 and the ideas on page 53 on *Releasing Anxiety* are more examples of ideas that are helpful as well. The website *ConquerAnxiety.com* is a good source for alternative treatments among many others that are out there.

Journaling

Recording daily events enables a person to track anxiety triggers. Things that may trigger anxiety might be certain activities, people, situations, times of the month, and even certain types of food. The key is to look for patterns when one is especially anxious and note what is going on at these times. Does there seem to be a pattern?

A great way to look for patterns with anxiety is to use a Day Chart. Pages 56-57 of this book clearly explain how to chart feelings on a daily basis. Clear patterns emerge as one charts or rates each morning, afternoon, and evening. When anxiety triggers are seen, appropriate changes can be made in one's routine and habits to reduce anxiety.

Scheduling

Schedule less—not more in life. This frees us to focus on what's important and makes it easier to get things done that matter the most. Perhaps the best stress reliever is knowing how to say no and setting boundaries in our day-to-day lives. Taking on too many responsibilities and activities only adds to the level of anxiety.

You may want to sit down with your child or teen and together work out a reasonable weekly schedule. By paring out energy drainers, your child or teen can use that energy to overcome anxiety. Finding a few activities that bring joy into life increases energy. Be sure to schedule an enjoyable activity each day. We all need things to which we can look forward.

Medications

When the previous approaches don't work or need a boost, certain medications can offer help. In fact a recent research trial of children and adolescents ages 6 to 17 showed promising results. Seventy-six percent of those taking the medication "Fluvoxamine®" for the treatment of anxiety disorders showed marked improvement (NIMH, 2001). None reported significant side effects. Side effects were mild to nonexistent for most. Antidepressants called selective serotonin reuptake inhibitors (SSRI) such as Prozac® work by preventing the brain from absorbing too much of the chemical serotonin. This helps improve mood. Another SSRI, Paxil®, has been approved by the Food and Drug Administration (FDA) specifically for the treatment of social-anxiety disorder. Zoloft® has been approved for OCD and panic disorder.

A new group of antidepressants called serotonin-norepinephrine reuptake inhibitors (SNRI's) target a second chemical in the brain called norepinephrine. Norepinephrine is secreted by the adrenal gland and plays a great role in how people respond to stress. The chemical norepinephrine is manipulated to control emotion and stabilize mood.

For more information you may refer to publications such as *Straight Talk about Psychiatric Medications for Kids* by Timothy E. Wilens, M.D. (1999).

What's Going On In The Brain?

Stress is an internal response to a stressor. A stressor is an external event or situation that places a physical or psychological demand on a person. When stress occurs, a virtual chain reaction occurs in the brain and throughout the body.

In the brain the thalamus processes and interprets the information and sends it to either the amygdala or to the cortex. Thus, the brain has two neural pathways when anxiety is experienced. The brain has an emergency route to the amygdala, the brain's fear center. The second and more circuitous route is to the cortex for more in-depth processing.

The amygdala quickly activates systems over the entire body for immediate action. In essence, this is like an alarm system going off. The classic fear response occurs which includes sweaty palms, increased blood pressure and heart rate, and an adrenaline rush.

The hippocampus, which learns and stores new memories, is also activated by the amygdala. Essentially, the hippocampus is a memory center. It stores new information from our senses that is attached to emotions.

Meanwhile the second pathway to the cortex is completed. The cortex recognizes that danger is present and logically figures out what to do about it. Once the prefrontal cortex assesses that the danger has subsided, it sends out a message to end the state of alert. It tells the amygdala that the danger has passed. The problem, however, for many people is that it is harder to turn off this fear response than it is to start it.

Research quoted in the article called *The Science of Anxiety,* from the June 10, 2002 issue of *Time* magazine "showed that the anxiety response isn't necessarily caused by an external threat; rather, it may be traced to a breakdown in the mechanism that signals the brain to stop responding" (Gorman, 2002, p. 53). The cause for some anxiety disorders may turn out to be an overactive amygdala while an underactive prefrontal cortex may cause others. The overactive amygdala may be analogous to a stuck accelerator and the underactive prefrontal cortex to failed brakes (Gorman). Scientists are also studying the bed nucleus of the stria terminalis (BNST). The BNST is a pea-sized cluster of neurons located near the amygdala. The BNST, "unlike the amygdala, which sets off an immediate burst of fear, perpetuates the fear response, causing the longer-term unease typical of anxiety" (Park, 2002, p. 51). It could be that the BNST is malfunctioning, and therefore causing lasting anxiety in some people.

A rich explanation of what happens where in the mind is found in *Straight Talk about Psychiatric Medications for Kids* by Timothy E. Wilens, M.D (1999). He also discusses in detail how psychiatric medications prescribed for children work in relation to the brain. Pages 25-33 of Wilens' book are particularly helpful.

Kids Have A Lot On Their Plates, Too

Y ou have no doubt heard an adult say something like, "What do kids have to worry about? You wait until they grow up! Then they'll have real stress." The fact of the matter is that kids  don't get to wait until adulthood to be stressed. This is most unfortunate but true as research indicates. Consider the following information.

A new study shows that from the 1950s to the present, stress and anxiety have affected more and more kids. Today children are suffering far more anxiety than any previous generation, leading some to call this the "Age of Anxiety." "Anxiety has increased substantially among children and college-age students, over three decades," says Jean M. Twenge, Ph.D., a psychologist with Case Western Reserve University in Cleveland, Ohio. Her research shows that the environment in which a child lives can have a large impact on feelings such as anxiety (Davis, 2000).

Twenge looked at research involving 40,000 college students and 12,000 children, aged 9-17, between 1952 and 1993. These kids grew up in all kinds of settings including cities, suburbs, and rural areas. Twenge found "steady and significantly large increases in anxiety levels" in children during this period (Davis, 2000).

Why Are Kids Worried And Anxious?

K ids cite all kinds of reasons behind their worries and fears. The following list is not an exhaustive list but is a good sample. How many anxiety producing factors might your child be facing?

Environmental Dangers

- Crime
- Community violence
- AIDS
- Worry about nuclear war
- Terrorism

Family Issues

- Separation and divorce of parents
- Moving to new locations
- Single-parenting
- Being away from family members
- Isolation and loneliness
- Family dysfunction
- Physical and verbal abuse
- Constant arguing
- Chronic illness in the family
- Loss of a family member

Economic Factors

- Parent's unemployment

- Poverty

School Problems

- Poor grades

- Learning disabilities

- Peer conflicts

- Isolation

All of these factors and more affect kids. These factors obviously affect adults, too, but how much more are kids affected who have even less control over their lives? Children and adolescents are especially vulnerable.

The bottom line is that lasting anxiety takes a large toll on all of us physically and mentally. Anxiety is linked to health problems such as asthma, heart disease, gastrointestinal problems, and depression among other things.

So What Can Grown-Ups Do To Help Kids?

As grown-ups it is our responsibility to meet our kids' needs and to set the best environment possible. Kids feel secure when adults set good boundaries and limits for them. Below are some practical tips to consider.

1. Limit violent media that leaves children with the perception that their neighborhood and world is unsafe.

2. Build good relationships so kids feel connected in their families and neighborhoods. Social relationships serve as a buffer against stress.

3. Listen and discuss your child's worries and fears.

4. Have realistic expectations about life. Movies and television can set up unrealistic expectations for kids in terms of appearance, jobs, wealth, and relationships. Trying to reach unreachable ideals can cause great anxiety. You cannot change a child's genetics, but you can change the media they watch, along with the quality of their relationships. It's difficult to change the entire society, but you can change society's impact on you and your family (Davis, 2000).

5. If your kid's anxiety and stress is not abating, get a professional to help him or her. As mentioned before, counselors and physicians can be of good help.

Other Factors Behind Anxiety With Children And Teens

Heredity and medical problems often contribute to problematic anxiety. Consider the following information and think about your child's possible genetic loading and medical issues. This is information again that is good to discuss with your kid's physician.

Genetics

There is a higher chance of an anxiety disorder in the parents, children and siblings of a person with an anxiety disorder than in the relatives of someone without an anxiety disorder. Studies of identical twins demonstrate varying but important degrees of genetic contributions to the development of anxiety disorders. For example, studies show 50% of patients with panic disorder have at least one relative affected with an anxiety disorder (Goldman, 2002).

Medical

The first thing to rule in or out with any apparent mental disorder is a physical problem. It is good to rule these things out first by having a complete physical done by your doctor. The following list of medical problems can create anxiety within a person. This is not a complete list, but all can have links to anxiety.

- Cardiovascular disease

- Lung disease

- Certain tumors

- Hyperthyroidism

- Infections

- Neurological disease

- Streptococcus (Scientists at the National Institute of Mental Health and elsewhere have recently found that some obsessive-compulsive disorders occur following infection or exposure to streptococcus bacteria) (*National Alliance for the Mentally Ill, 2001*).

How The Body Reacts To Ongoing Stress And Anxiety:
Possible Places Where Stress And Anxiety May Attack Us

Where does anxiety and stress affect the body? Each person is affected differently. It is important to "listen to our bodies." Just as an athlete pays attention to his or her body in order to know how hard to push physical limits, people in general can tell a lot by paying attention to what is happening physically. When some of the problems illustrated here persist regularly, the body is sending out warning signals. Stress over a prolonged period will begin to break people down physically. Does your child experience any of the following problems on a regular basis?

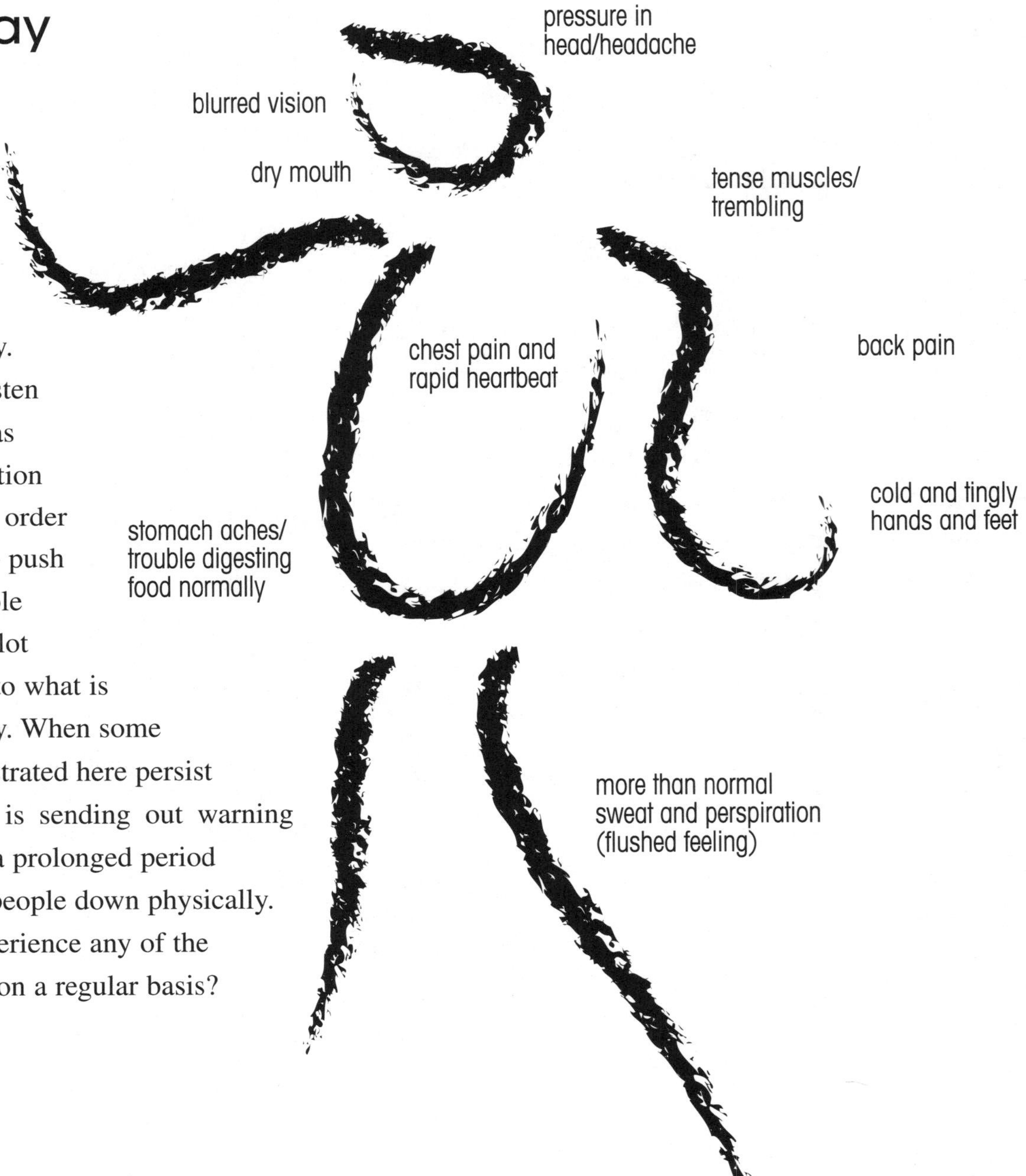

pressure in head/headache

blurred vision

dry mouth

tense muscles/ trembling

chest pain and rapid heartbeat

back pain

cold and tingly hands and feet

stomach aches/ trouble digesting food normally

more than normal sweat and perspiration (flushed feeling)

Other Possible Symptoms Of Ongoing Stress & Anxiety Found In Children And Adolescents

The following are more possible symptoms of childhood and adolescent anxiety and stress. This list accents behavior and emotional changes that can occur when a child or teen is distressed. Looking at the intensity, frequency, and duration of behaviors and certain emotions are key. Does your child have any of these symptoms?

- Changes in eating patterns (eating more than normal or not eating at all)

- Sleep problems (sleeping too much or too little)

- Feeling restless—unable to wind down

- Losing interest in doing normal activities

- Feeling worthless and thinking bad thoughts about yourself and your situation

- Difficulty concentrating

- Feeling irritable and upset

- Feeling fatigued or out of energy to cope

- Withdrawal—avoiding people, places, and situations

- Self-medicating/using alcohol and other substances

- Changes in school performance or poor grades

- Hyperactivity

- Regular nightmares

- Aggressive behavior/not obeying adults in charge

- Excessive worry and trying to do things perfectly

- Outbursts of anger

- Depression—long-lasting sad or hopeless feelings

- Complaints of physical illnesses, aches, and pains

Ten Common Fears Kids Face With Suggestions On How Grown-ups Can Help

The following are a few examples of how parents and helping professionals can help with specific fears that children and teens encounter. This is a short list with a specific suggestion for each. Pages 71-82 in the kids' section of this book provide many more examples of common fears and specific strategies to overcome various fears. We highly encourage you and your child or teen to read this part of the book for many more creative coping strategies that are written in "kid friendly" terms.

1. Sleeping Alone in Own Room

Suggestion: If you are in this situation, likely your child is sleeping in the parent(s)' bedroom. A good way to work toward getting your child in his/her own room is the "sleeping bag method." This method involves having your child sleep in his/her sleeping bag while moving steadily from location to location ever closer to his/her bedroom. Each night the child moves at least a few feet toward the goal. Once momentum is gained, this process tends to move right along.

2. Being Afraid of the Dark

Suggestion: Darkness is an innate fear with many kids. As with most fears, working on it gradually is wise. "The Dimmer Method" is one such approach. Find a light (preferably a night light) that has a dimmer switch. Dim the light to a comfortable level for your child making it as conducive for sleep as possible. Each night dim the light a little more. It may take several weeks, but sooner or later your child should be conditioned to minimal light and eventually total darkness.

3. Monsters and Other Scary Imaginary Beings

Suggestion: Locate an empty spray bottle and label it "Monster Spray." Also, get a small flashlight. Explain to your child that this "monster spray bottle" will keep any monsters away. Explain that just in case you think you see one, use your flashlight to prove that the monster spray is working. It always does.

4. Being Overwhelmed—Too Much to Do

Suggestion: Lou Holtz in his book *Winning Every Day* emphasizes the acronym **WIN**. This stands for **W**hat's **I**mportant **N**ow (1999). When facing daunting tasks, teach the **WIN** acronym to your child. This will help him/her to set priorities and take one positive step after another when climbing the proverbial mountain.

5. Separating from Trusted Adults

Suggestion: The "Magic Number Check Up" works well for separation anxiety. Simply say to your child that he or she will need to separate from you or another trusted adult for a magic number of minutes. For example, have the child go alone upstairs to his or her room for an agreed upon time period. Make sure the child has some control in terms of how many minutes. This "magic number" for example may be only one or two minutes for starters. The magic number grows steadily until separation from trusted persons is reasonably comfortable. When the magic number reaches ten minutes to fifteen minutes, usually the battle has been won!

6. School Phobia

Suggestion: The "School Mapping" works well for kids reluctant to go into the school building. Have the student draw a map or route from the point of drop-off outside of school to his or her homeroom. Now ask the student to set up goals in terms of walking alone to increasingly farther distances into the school. Note the progress being made on the map. Once the child or teen gets to the designated spot or goal, an adult or friend can assist him or her to the classroom. Over time, complete independence is gained.

For kids with extreme school phobia, a partial schedule may be necessary. Staying at school for short periods and gradually increasing the time stayed is sometimes necessary. In these cases, a medical excuse is normally needed from the child's or teen's physician.

7. Test Anxiety

Suggestion: You may have heard of the expression, "I don't give one iota about it." While we don't want kids to be careless about tests, less anxiety is desired. Teach the meaning of the secret code word **IOTA**. This stands for, "**I**t's **O**nly a **T**est **A**nyway." By putting tests into proper perspective, children and teens will be less likely to stress out. Remember, kids take their cues from the adults in their lives. Be positive and make sure that we, as adults, aren't adding to the anxiety about tests.

8. Bullies

Suggestion: Teaching kids assertiveness skills is key. Confident kids tend to get picked on less. Things like having a steady and confident gait and eye contact go a long way. Speaking up without being abrasive or overly confrontational is also a skill to teach kids. Kids should also be encouraged to develop a support system. Having a **good group** "to hang with" and having **trusted adults** that are always there to help is a necessity. A good relationship with at least one adult who has the power to intervene can make all the difference. Help kids who are feeling intimidated to write an actual list of "go to" people who can help them when life gets rough.

9. Germs/Sickness

Suggestion: **Desensitizing** or getting more and more used to situations or things is in play here. For example, if your child or teen is afraid of certain places or things for fear of catching germs, he or she must be challenged to approach and gradually conquer these feelings. Let's say one is afraid of going to the local mall due to being exposed to people with possible germs. Start by riding to the mall and coming home. Next, walk up to the mall door and leave. Then, walk inside briefly and walk out. Follow this with going into a store and eventually making a purchase. Gradual exposure to the feared stimulus with the child guiding the process with the adult's input works well. Once again, in many of these situations, medical issues may be in play, so it is wise to be working in conjunction with a physician and psychotherapist.

10. Terrorism

Suggestion: Parents and other adults need to limit exposure to the media. Kids are often exposed to situations and details through the media with which they are unable to cope. Try these three ideas.

a. Give kids the basic facts. Reduce T.M.I. (too much information).

b. Process what has happened while allowing kids to express their feelings. Listen well. Summarize and clarify what the child is saying and reflect his/her feelings.

c. Get back on the normal routine as soon as possible. Being in the normal routine provides a sense of stability.

Most importantly, remember that kids take their cues from the adults around them. If the adult(s) around them are calm and under control, the kids are likely to follow.

Good Help Is Out There

The following are some wonderful websites and books. Good information and encouragement about anxiety problems can be found in many places. The following lists will give you a good running start. Also, remember some of the best help is often available locally. Contacting mental health professionals and physicians is highly encouraged.

Where to look for help on the Web

There are many wonderful sources of information and support, many of which can be found on the Internet or in your community's libraries. Below are several good Internet starting points. Additionally, your physician, nurse, clergyperson or counselor can be a good source of information.

American Academy of Child and Adolescent Psychiatry ......*www.aacap.org*

American Psychiatric Association...............................*www.psych.org*

American Psychological Association ....*www.apa.org*

Anxiety Disorders Association of America.............*www.adaa.org*

Anxiety Disorders in Children.............. *www.keepkidshealthy.com*

Federation of Families for Children's Mental Health ....*www.ffcmh.org*

Freedom From Fear ....*www.freedomfromfear.com*

Head Start Mental Health Resources ....*www.hskids-tmsc.org*

Knowledge Exchange Network (800-789-2647) ....*www.mentalhealth.org*

National Institute of Mental Health ....*www.nih.gov*

National Mental Health Association (800-969-NMHA) ....*www.nmha.org*

Books

Helping Your Anxious Child: A Step-by-Step Guide for Parents by Ronald Rapee, New Harbinger Publications, 2000.

Keys to Parenting Your Anxious Child by Katharina Manassis, Barron's Educational Series, 1996.

Section 2
For Kids

(but grown-ups can read it, too!)

Stuff For Kids To Know About Anxiety & Stress

(suggested grade levels preK-5)

Everyone has anxiety and stress. Anxiety is worry or fear about things that may happen. Kids often feel a little nervous about an upcoming test for example. Or one might feel afraid of a thunderstorm. These are normal types of anxiety.

Anxiety is only a real problem when it is strong and lasts a long time. When strong worries and fears go on and on, this puts stress on our bodies and minds.

Stress is strain on the body and mind. Things like tense muscles, sweating a lot, heart pounding, and trouble sitting still happen when one is under stress.

About one in every eight people has strong and lasting worries and fears called Anxiety Disorders. When one has an Anxiety Disorder, it is a good idea to see a doctor and a counselor for help.

This book is all about helping kids understand more about anxiety problems with tips on how to feel better. Please continue reading for some helpful ideas starting on page 34. Good luck as you try these tips to overcome anxiety.

Stuff For Teens To Know About Anxiety & Stress

(Suggested grade levels 6-12)

**We all have it.
Some have more of it.
It is called anxiety and stress.**

Stress is great strain on the body and mind. Too much anxiety can cause headaches, stomachaches, tense muscles, chest pain, tiredness and other types of stress on the body and mind. Anxiety is strong and overwhelming worry or fear. If anxiety lasts on and on, it can become an anxiety disorder. When anxiety gets in the way of normal living, this is called an anxiety disorder. The following are common types of anxiety disorders that people sometimes experience.

Separation Anxiety—Being overly worried about being away from trusted adults. Unnecessary worry about something happening to parents, not being able to sleep in one's own bed, and trouble going to school are examples of separation anxiety.

Panic Disorder—Having chest pains, rapid heartbeat, difficulty breathing, a fear of losing control or even dying.

Phobias—Having a great fear of specific things and situations such as animals, insects, storms, heights, elevators, etc.

Obsessive-Compulsive Disorder—Constant worry about specific things such as germs, doing something wrong, putting things in order, etc. along with constantly washing hands, double checking, repeating words, etc.

Post-traumatic Stress Disorder—Replaying a scary event over and over in the mind. Repeated flashbacks and scary dreams that seem real.

Generalized Anxiety Disorder—Regular, ongoing worry about life. Difficulty controlling feelings of worry and anxiety.

These disorders often need to be treated with therapy (counseling) and medicine. Therapy helps individuals to understand anxiety and to learn good ways to cope with it. Medicines, such as Prozac® and Zoloft®, are used to help balance chemicals in the brain. As chemicals in the brain such as serotonin are controlled, feelings of anxiety are often greatly reduced.

Most people do not have a full-blown type of anxiety disorder, but it is not unusual to have one. In fact 13% or about 1 in 8 children and teens have anxiety disorders. All kids face anxiety and stress to some degree, so it is wise for everyone to learn some good ways to deal with it. In the pages ahead, you will learn some practical coping strategies and activities. Some of the ideas and activities may seem a little unusual, but they absolutely work, especially if you practice them regularly. Please read on and see which ones may be of help to you. Good luck as you put them to use.

Strategy 1:
Discovering The Secret
Of Overcoming Fears

(suggested grade levels PreK-4)

The Defeat of the Great
Drizzlenerd

A Story for Big & Little Kids
in Overcoming Fears & Phobias

Once upon a time long, long ago there was a land called Scareee.
The people of this land lived in fear because of a
strange looking monster named the Drizzlenerd.
As you can see, the Drizzlenerd was big and UGLY!

The people in the Land of Scareee would often stay in their
homes where they would be safe. However, from time to time,
the people would need to travel between their two main cities.

The two towns were called Fear and Trepidation (tre-pə-dā-shən).

Some who dared to travel did not return.

No one knew for sure what happened to them.

One day a young girl named Cary had to travel between the towns of Fear and Trepidation to bring medicine to a friend who was very sick.

Cary was almost halfway there when she heard the unmistakable sound of the great Drizzlenerd.

The Drizzlenerd would snort so loudly that it could be heard all around.

Cary trembled with fear and thought about running away from the sound of the Drizzlenerd.

It sounded closer and closer but was still out of sight.

Cary had heard that running
from the great Drizzlenerd
would only draw its attention,
which meant certain doom.

So Cary stood still
hoping not to be noticed.

But no such luck!

The great monster
had spotted Cary.

Her only choice was to face this monster.
Cary thought quickly as the great Drizzlenerd
was now in sight and getting closer and closer.

Remembering she always carried a mirror in her purse, Cary took it out. It was a good-sized mirror. With mirror in hand, Cary ran toward the great Drizzlenerd. The onrushing person surprised the monster.

Just outside of an arm's length from the monster, Cary flashed the mirror across the bright sky toward the great Drizzlenerd.

The great monster, curious as to what this mirror was, looked into it.

For the first time the Drizzlenerd saw his own reflection.

At the sight of his grotesque and hideous face, the great Drizzlenerd turned and lumbered away.

He was scared of his own ugly looks.

Cary's bravery and quick thinking saved her life and the lives of many others as it turned out.

From that day on, the people of the Land of Scareee
freely traveled everywhere with mirrors in hand.

Just the sight of a mirror would send
the monster running for cover.

In fact, the name of their fair land was changed
from Scareee to Careee in honor of this young
person's courage and clear thinking.

The great Drizzlenerd would never be a menace again for the

good folks of Careee who lived happily ever after.

The End

The moral of the story is to always face problems and situations and not to run away from them.

To have victory, we must be brave and smart.

Channels

(grade levels PreK-4)

Think of your brain as being like a television (T.V.) with three channels. Just as a T.V. has different images or pictures on each channel, the brain has different ways of thinking about life's situations. You can picture situations and things in life in a good or bad way. The choice is yours.

Channel One in your brain is called **cloudy mind.** The cloudy brain channel looks at things in the worst way. You let things bother you, and you don't feel good about yourself. You can't think clearly and let things or situations ruin your day. People who are in their cloudy minds get mad, worried, or upset and stay upset.

Now think about what you would do if you were watching a T.V. show and you didn't like it. Let's say the program was too scary. What would you do? Of course, you would change the channel. In a similar way, when your brain is stuck in your cloudy mind, you can choose to change the channel. Imagine that you have a remote control for your brain. You can change to channel two or three.

Channel two is the **sunny mind.** The sunny brain channel is when you think clearly. You don't let things bother you (at least not for long) and you feel good about yourself. You have a good ability to handle what comes your way even when things don't go right.

Channel three is the **rainbow mind.** When you are on the rainbow channel, your brain is full of good ideas. You can think of great ideas to solve problems in your life. You can solve not only hard math problems but personal problems as well.

Always remember that you can control your way of thinking. You can choose to stay in channels two and three. If you find yourself in your cloudy mind, as we all do at times, remember you can change the channel any time you wish. Make a special effort to stay tuned to channels two and three, and you'll be more relaxed and smarter than ever.

Here are some examples of the three brain channels.

Situation: **You have a big test coming up soon.**

1. *Cloudy Mind—*

   "I know I'm going to mess up."

2. *Sunny Mind—*

   "I know the test will be hard, but I'll do all right."

3. *Rainbow Mind—"*

   I'll get with my friend who is real smart about this stuff. We'll study together, and then I know I'll be ready for the test."

Situation: **You're home alone, and you hear a strange noise.**

1. *Cloudy Mind—*

   "I just know someone is trying to break into our house."

2. *Sunny Mind—*

   "I heard a noise, but I always hear noises around here especially when the wind is blowing. It's probably nothing."

3. *Rainbow Mind—*

   "I'll check it out and see what the noise is. Then I'll know that everything is fine."

Strategy 3:
R and R

(suggested grade levels PreK-4)

A little rest and relaxation can go a long way to help with stress and anxiety. Try these techniques when you feel tension coming on.

The Big Sponge

This relaxation technique involves imagining that you are a sponge. To squeeze out stress and tension, tighten all your muscles (without hurting yourself) and silently count slowly to five. Then relax all your muscles for a few seconds and repeat this over and over. As you tense and relax your muscles, you will wring out more and more stress and anxiety.

Lemon Squeezing

Imagine you are making lemonade by squeezing out fresh lemons. Use a couple of stress balls or imaginary lemons and tightly squeeze both fists. Squeeze to a count of three or so, and then relax for a few seconds. As you squeeze your fists tightly over and over, you are getting rid of any stress or bitterness.

The Big Balloon

Imagine that your stomach is a balloon. Breathe in slowly through your nose and watch your stomach (balloon) expand. Hold that breath to the count of three, and then breathe out slowly through your mouth. Do this several times and watch your stress blow away.

One-Minute Vacation

As you have some free time after a stressful day, give yourself a minute or two to daydream a bit. Imagine a favorite place or thing you like to do that is relaxing and enjoyable. Some examples might be playing at the beach, hiking in the mountains, playing a favorite sport, etc. Pretend you are there and imagine what it looks like, smells like, feels like, sounds like, etc.

Strategy 4: List Therapy

(suggested grade levels PreK-4)

Most of us feel uncomfortable if not downright afraid of new situations and things. This is normal. Whether it is going on a roller coaster, giving an oral report in front of a class, or being afraid of the dark, we all have worries and fears. A good way to overcome such fears is to face them one by one. As you are successful in taking even small steps to overcome fears and general anxiety, list or write down your accomplishments. In this way, you can see your progress and build on it.

Suppose you are a very shy person. Keeping a list on how you are learning to be more outgoing is helpful. Consider the following list of accomplishments for overcoming shyness.

1. Ordering my own food at a restaurant.

2. Answering a question in class.

3. Joining in and playing with a group of classmates.

4. Working a math problem at the board.

5. Asking for help when lost.

6. Going to an overnight birthday party.

7. Other _____

This list could go on and on, but you get the idea. As momentum is built, it is hard to stop. You may want to start your own list of brave things you are doing.

Strategy 5:
Dream Planning

(suggested grade levels PreK-12)

Many people report having trouble getting to sleep and having nightmares. Dream rehearsal or dream planning when done on a regular basis can change things for the better. This technique tends to be very effective, but it must become a habit.

The last thing a person thinks about before going to sleep has the most effect on how well he or she rests. If a person is thinking about stressful things, unpleasant dreams and trouble going to sleep are likely. Sometimes people are even unaware of these thoughts. To change all this, one plans what he or she would like to dream. By focusing on pleasant thoughts, the chances of falling asleep quickly and having good dreams are greatly improved. Planning how you want your dream to go each night is a way of training the brain to think positively. Good thoughts help the body and brain to relax.

While practicing dream planning, nightmares are still possible, especially when you first start. If this occurs, just tell yourself, "This isn't the way my dream is supposed to go." Then simply go back to the dream you planned. More and more, your sleep and dreams will improve as you stick with dream planning.

It is said that it takes 21 days to form a new habit. By using dream planning for 21 straight days, nightmares and staying awake at bedtime should give way to good sleep. Sweet dreams!

Activity: Draw or write down how you want your dream to go for tonight. You may want to draw or briefly write it out on paper for the next several nights.

My Drawing of Tonight's Dream:

My Story of Tonight's Dream:

_____

_____

_____

_____

_____

_____

_____

_____

Strategy 6:
RASing Your Feelings
(suggested grade levels 2-6)

When it comes to feelings, you have all kinds. It is important to know how to handle feelings. The word **RAS** is another secret code word worth remembering. It can remind you of three important things to do with your feelings.

"R" stands for Recognize Your Feelings

Recognize means to know or to think about your feelings. You have two types of feelings. Here are some examples under each type.

Pleasant Feelings *(Feelings we like)*	Unpleasant Feelings *(Feelings we don't like)*
happy	sad
excited	mad
surprised	frustrated
loved	disappointed
confident	scared
hopeful	guilty
	embarrassed
	worried

Recognizing or knowing what feelings you have is very important. Throughout each day, stop for a minute and listen to your feelings. Ask, how am I feeling right now? Your body and mind will tell you.

"A" stands for Accept Your Feelings

Accept means that your feelings are always O.K. Accept means to take your feelings as they are. There is nothing wrong with feeling the way you do. Feelings are a part of you, and they are O.K.

"S" stands for Share Your Feelings

Feelings are to be **shared** with others. Talking to people you trust about your feelings is a wonderful way to express your feelings. Feelings are not to be kept inside. You just feel better when you talk to others about your feelings. With whom can you share your feelings? Try to think of at least three people whom you believe can be trusted with your deepest feelings.

Adapted with permission from Frank, K. and Smith-Rex, S., (1996), *Getting Over the Blues: A Kid's Guide to Understanding and Coping with Unpleasant Feelings and Depression.* Minneapolis, MN: Educational Media.

Strategy 7:
Chill Out Plan

(suggested grade levels 2-8)

To find a balance in our lives, it is a good idea to have a **C.O.P.** A C.O.P. is short for **C**hill **O**ut **P**lan. This is a plan where one chooses a few healthy things to do when anxiety arises. Below is a list of ideas kids have shared that have helped them to get over upset feelings. *Choose at least three or four things that you can do to chill out the next time you get anxious.* The more you use your C.O.P., the better you'll get at handling anxiety and other unpleasant feelings. Your C.O.P. will become automatic after a while, so practice, practice, practice.

Ideas for Chill Out Plan

1. Talk to someone you trust

2. Conflict management
   (talk it out if you are having a problem with another person as soon as possible)

3. Count to ten or higher to calm down

4. Hit a pillow or punching bag

5. Positive self-talk
   (Use clear messages—see page 58)

6. Tense and relax your muscles

7. Squeeze a ball

8. Read a book

9. Pray about it

10. Listen to music

11. Exercise

12. Take a time out

13. Take a deep breath

14. Write in a journal

15. Take a one-minute vacation
    (While not in class, imagine going to a favorite spot or doing a favorite activity.)

16. Enjoy a pet

17. Draw or paint your feelings

My Chill Out Plan

List three to five ideas you can do to chill out when you are stressed.

1. _____

2. _____

3. _____

4. _____

5. _____

Adapted with permission from Frank, K. and Smith-Rex, S., (1996), *Getting Over the Blues: A Kid's Guide to Understanding and Coping with Unpleasant Feelings and Depression.* Minneapolis, MN: Educational Media.

Strategy 8:
Releasing Anxiety
(suggested grade levels 2-12)

Create your own bag of tricks to release anxiety. Collect things such as modeling dough, squeeze balls, color markers and drawing paper, sand timer, stress control cards, a good book, etc. Anything goes as long as it is safe and appropriate. As these items are used, anxiety melts away. It's fun, too.

Actually one of the best collections of stuff is found in the "Chill Out Bag" produced by Youthlight, Inc. (Bowman, 1997). Items in the chill out bag include an anger (stress) control card, Laugh Bag, Scream Sack, Sand Timer, Tension Ball, Sponge Ball, "Stress Doh," and PunchBall. The Chill Out Bag may be ordered at (800) 209-9774. Have some fun!

Strategy 9:
FADD
(suggested grade levels 5-12)

Another way of remembering how to overcome fears is to use this secret code word called **FADD**. It stands for:

F **ace the problem or situation.**
Don't run away from it.

A **ccept or take on the problem or situation.**
It probably isn't going to just go away. Deal with it.

D **ecide what to do.**
Think of smart things to do.
Use your brain power and don't be afraid to seek help from others.

D **o it.**
Good things happen when you act wisely on your plan. Have the courage to follow through on your plan.

Make a Plan
Work through the steps below to overcome what bothers you.

Face it ⟶ Accept it

Write down the problem or situation that is causing anxiety for you.

_____

Decide what to do ⟶ Do it

Write down your best ideas to cope or deal with your problem or situation.

_____

_____

Strategy 10:
ANT Killing

(suggested grade levels 4-12)

People so often have thoughts that cause problems for them. Thoughts like, "It's terrible; I can't stand it; Everything is awful;" etc. cause us problems. These types of thoughts bring about unhappy and anxious feelings. If left unnoticed, these unhelpful thoughts become a bad habit. We call them **ANTS**, which stands for **A**utomatic **N**egative **T**houghts.

A utomatic ....instant

N egative ....bad

T houghts ....ideas

Automatic **N**egative **T**houghts are bad or unhelpful ideas that just happen over and over in our minds.

Like ants, they can cover you in no time and cause you to be miserable. Instead of being miserable, we want you to become **ANT** killers. **ANT** killing involves catching and killing your negative thoughts as you notice them. In this way, you don't allow yourself to think in negative, unhelpful ways. Instead learn to replace them with good thoughts that help you to work out problems and feel better about yourself.

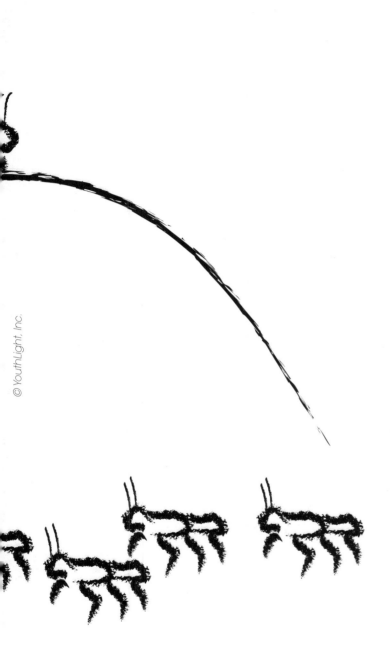

The following is a list of thoughts from the ANT hill. Try to catch these thoughts before you start to believe them. Circle any automatic negative thoughts which you have had that need to be killed.

ANT Hill

1. It's just awful.

2. I can't stand it.

3. It's just too scary.

4. I'll just die if it doesn't go my way.

5. I can't handle it.

6. I'll only be happy when things change.

7. If only things were different, I'd feel better.

8. This is the worst thing.

9. It must work out.

10. It just figures this would happen.

11. It shouldn't be this way.

12. Life is always bad.

13. Everything is just awful.

14. It's impossible.

15. This could only happen to me.

Notice the circled words. Become aware of the **ANTS** you have and become an **ANT** killer.

Adapted with permission from Frank, K. and Smith-Rex, S., (1996), *Getting Over the Blues: A Kid's Guide to Understanding and Coping with Unpleasant Feelings and Depression.* Minneapolis, MN: Educational Media.

Strategy 11:
Charting My Feelings

(suggested grade levels 4-12)

It is important to pay attention to your feelings each day. One good way to do this is to keep a **Day Chart** for your feelings. Using a Day Chart helps you to see patterns in your emotions. You will be able to note events or situations that bring about pleasant or unpleasant feelings. You will also be more aware of slumps. Slumps are periods of several days when you are having unpleasant feelings. In such cases, we recommend that you talk to people you trust to help turn your feelings around. A good rule of thumb is that after two days of unpleasant feelings, you should seek out someone in your support system with whom you can discuss your situation and feelings.

The following is a made-up example of a Day Chart. Notice the scale of 1 to 10 to rate your feelings, which is done three times daily. Also, an average score is figured for the three parts of the day. (Just add up your three scores for morning, afternoon, and evening and then divide by three. Don't worry about remainders.)

Make several copies of the blank Day Chart on the next page and keep track of how your days are going. As we mentioned earlier, if you see a pattern of low scores, talk it over with someone you trust. As you learn ways to cope and work out problems, your score is bound to rise.

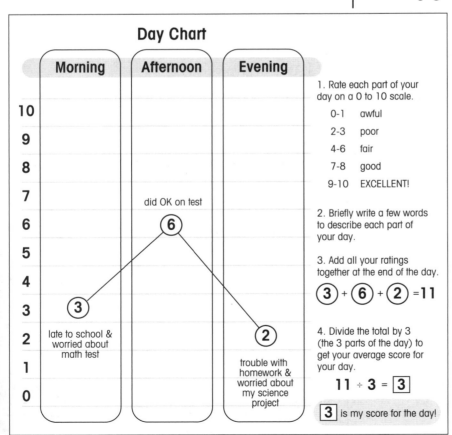

Day Chart

1. Rate each part of your day on a 0 to 10 scale.

0-1	awful
2-3	poor
4-6	fair
7-8	good
9-10	EXCELLENT!

2. Briefly write a few words to describe each part of your day.

3. Add all your ratings together at the end of the day.

$$3 + 6 + 2 = 11$$

4. Divide the total by 3 (the 3 parts of the day) to get your average score for your day.

$$11 \div 3 = 3$$

3 is my score for the day!

Adapted with permission from Frank, K. and Smith-Rex, S., (1996), *Getting Over the Blues: A Kid's Guide to Understanding and Coping with Unpleasant Feelings and Depression.* Minneapolis, MN: Educational Media.

Day Chart

Morning	Afternoon	Evening

10
9
8
7
6
5
4
3
2
1
0

Today's Date

1. Rate each part of your day on a 0 to 10 scale.

0-1	awful
2-3	poor
4-6	fair
7-8	good
9-10	EXCELLENT!

2. Briefly write a few words to describe each part of your day.

3. Add all your ratings together at the end of the day.

◯ + ◯ + ◯ = ___

4. Divide the total by 3 (the 3 parts of the day) to get your average score for your day.

___ ÷ **3** = ☐

☐ is my score for the day!

Strategy 12:
Clear VS. Muddy Messages

(suggested grade levels 4-12)

One of the best ways to overcome anxiety is to change your way of thinking. Your thinking can help or hurt you. You have basically two ways of thinking about yourself and the things that happen to you. We call them muddy messages and clear messages.

Muddy messages are thoughts that cause you to feel badly about yourself. You feel upset inside and things bother you.

Clear messages are just the opposite. These thoughts make you feel good about yourself and handle what comes your way. You feel at peace inside and things don't bother you, at least not for long.

Here are some examples of clear versus muddy thinking.

Event: *You have to give a speech.*

Muddy Message	Clear Message
I just know I'm going to "choke."	I'll just do my best. It doesn't have to be perfect.

Event: *You're going to camp for the first time.*

Muddy Message	Clear Message
I'll never make the whole week.	I'll have to be brave. Things will work out.

This is called **self-talk**. What you say to yourself makes all the difference. To feel good about yourself, it is important to think good thoughts. Good thoughts equal positive feelings. Think of a situation you are facing. How are your messages, clear or muddy? What is a clear message you can give yourself about a situation you are facing now?

Adapted with permission from Frank, K. and Smith-Rex, S., (1996), *Getting Over the Blues: A Kid's Guide to Understanding and Coping with Unpleasant Feelings and Depression.* Minneapolis, MN: Educational Media.

Strategy 13:
The Three R's

(suggested grade levels 4-12)

The Three R's: Recognizing, Reality Checking and Reframing

How we think about ourselves and the things that happen to us is key. Our perceptions (how we're looking at things) are often more important than the event that is happening to us. While a person may not be able to control a lot of things that happen such as parents' divorce, moving, teasing, and so forth, we can always control our thinking. Our thoughts are very powerful and often make the difference between coping (handling the situation in a good way) and not coping (not handling the situation well).

Recognizing Thoughts

Clear thinking involves giving yourself permission to stop and think. This involves recognizing your thoughts and feelings.

Stop and ask yourself a couple of questions.

1. Why am I feeling the way I am?

2. What exactly are my thoughts about this situation?

For example, suppose you just moved to a new school. Why am I feeling so nervous? Answer: I'm afraid no one will like me. What are my thoughts? "It will be just awful if I don't make a friend right away."

Reality Checking

Next, do some reality checking. Ask yourself the following question to see if you are looking at the situation as it **really is**.

• What proof (evidence) is there to believe this?

• In the case above, is there any real reason I won't be liked? No.

• Would it be awful to not make a friend right away? No, good friendships often take time and effort.

Reframing Thoughts

Now that I've caught some of my negative thoughts, I can try reframing. Reframing involves looking at the situation in the best way possible. This is called positive thinking. Ask yourself one more question to start to get yourself thinking positively.

• What is the best way to think about this situation?

Answer: I'll just be myself and look for a decent person or group to hang with.

Event:

Moving to a new school.

My Situation *(event that is happening):* _____

_____

_____

Recognizing My Thinking:
(What, if any, negative thoughts do I have?)

example: "It's awful;" "I can't stand it;"
"It's hopeless," etc.

My Negative Thoughts: _____

_____

_____

Reality Checking:
(What proof is there to believe this?)

example: "There is no proof that the situation
can't be handled. It's not the end of the
world, but rather it's a big challenge."

Reality: _____

_____

_____

Reframing My Thinking:
(What is the best way to think about this?)

example: "No one said it would be easy, but I
can work through this;" "I'll give it
my best shot."

New Thoughts: _____

_____

_____

**Apply the 3 R's to your life.
Check your thoughts and
think constructively.**

Adapted with permission from Frank, K. and Smith-Rex, S., (1996), *Getting Over the Blues: A Kid's Guide to Understanding and Coping with Unpleasant Feelings and Depression.* Minneapolis, MN: Educational Media.

Strategy 14:
Magic Button
(suggested grade levels 4-12)

Your five senses of smelling, tasting, seeing, hearing and touching work closely with your mind. Not only do your senses send important messages to your brain, they help create feelings. These feelings happen largely as a result of past experiences. For example, when you see a dog, your mind will recall past experiences involving dogs. These experiences may have been good, such as remembering times of playing with your favorite pet, or bad, such as being chased or bitten by a dog. Therefore, your feelings may be pleasant (happy, warm, etc.) or unpleasant (frightened, worried, etc.) depending on your experiences. Your mind has an amazing ability to bring back feelings of the past when situations occur. Think about the following situations and notice what feelings happen within yourself.

Event	My Feelings
Listening to waves at the beach	_____
Hearing a bee fly nearby	_____ _____
Exercising	_____ _____
Going to school	_____ _____
Eating a pizza with friends	_____ _____

Notice how certain feelings, some of them strong emotions, occurred. As stated earlier, the brain brings back feelings from the past. We can use this connection between your mind and senses to our advantage in order to relax and to improve our feelings. We call this "magic button." While it's really **not** magical, it seems like it is because depressed, anxious, and unhappy feelings can be washed away and replaced with happy and calm feelings.

Think of your brain as a computer that can be programmed by your sense of touch and by using your imagination. You pair or put together a mental image or picture in your mind with the sense of touch. There are a few steps in order to make this thing we call "magic button" work. First, list the types of feelings you would like to have. For example, happy, calm, confident, etc.

1. _____

2. _____

3. _____

Next, focus on using your imagination. Think of good experiences of the past or imagine experiences you would like to have. Center your imagination around experiences that help create or make the feelings you would like to have. Using the list of feelings you would like to have, choose one feeling or possibly two feelings.

For example: Relaxed   Peaceful

Now, think of five to ten good experiences that help bring about the exact feelings you want.

For example:

Specific feeling(s) chosen	Good experiences
Relaxed	Calling a friend on the phone
Peaceful	Hiking in the mountains
	Riding my bike on the bike path
	Eating pizza with friends
	Watching a favorite TV show

Now, choose your own specific feeling(s) and list your good experiences.

My specific feeling(s) that I would like to have:

_____

_____

_____

My good experiences *(List at least five)*:

_____

_____

_____

_____

_____

_____

At this point, we will "pair" or put together your sense of touch with the good experiences you've listed. As mentioned earlier, we call this "magic button." You will now need to choose a "magic button." Your magic button is simply a touch. It can be a touch on your elbow, knee, hip, etc. It can be a wiggle of a toe or finger. You decide for yourself. **The only rule is that you do the exact touch each time for the same length of time.** For example, you might wiggle your big toe three times or touch your elbow for three seconds. Again, the important thing to keep in mind is using your "magic button" the same way each time. Also, choose a magic button that is not very noticeable to others.

At this time, think of your "magic button" and write it down below.

My Magic Button: _____

_____

Now, you are ready to "pair" your "magic button" with your good experiences that you listed before. To do this, simply picture your good experiences. When you experience the pleasant feelings you desire, push your magic button. Continue visualizing or picturing these good experiences over and over. When your desired feelings grow strong, push your magic button. As you practice this on a regular basis, more and more pleasant feelings are experienced and etched into the mind. Once the connection between your magic button and feelings is made, you may use your magic button to bring about the feelings you want in seconds.

Suppose you've been practicing the use of your magic button for several days while picturing in your mind good experiences. When faced with unhappy feelings such as fear, you can push your magic button and replace these feelings with the ones you want. This usually occurs within seconds. The key is to practice, practice, practice, so your magic button can turn your feelings around automatically. Also, note that you can have different magic buttons for different feelings that you desire to have. Just use the same steps that we'll summarize at the end of this section. Some examples of magic buttons and specific feelings follow on the next page.

Specific Feelings	Magic Button
Happy	Touch knee
Confident (*good feeling about myself*)	Wiggle toe two times
Excited (*full of energy*)	Hold wrist

These, of course, are just examples. Some people have two or three magic buttons. Begin with one for starters. Once your first magic button is working well, you may want to work on another. Good luck as you try the steps of magic button that we will now summarize. Many have found this to be a powerful way of overcoming unpleasant feelings.

Summary of Magic Button Steps

1. Think of a specific feeling you want to have.

2. Make a list of good experiences you've had or would like to have that would help bring about the feeling you want.

3. Choose a magic button. Make sure your magic button touch or movement is the same each time.

4. Picture in your mind the good experiences you've listed. When your pleasant feeling is strong, push your magic button.

5. Practice step four regularly. The magic button connection to your desired feelings will become automatic.

6. Use your magic button during periods of time when you are having unpleasant feelings. This will wash them away and replace them with the pleasant feeling you want.

Adapted with permission from Frank, K. and Smith-Rex, S., (1996), *Getting Over the Blues: A Kid's Guide to Understanding and Coping with Unpleasant Feelings and Depression*. Minneapolis, MN: Educational Media.

Strategy 15:
Back Burner/ Front Burner
(suggested grade levels 4-12)

Listing Problem Areas or Life's Struggles

In order to take control of your life you need to decide which of your personal worries are within or out of your control. The first step in doing this is to actually list the things that stress you. Think for a few minutes and write down some of your worries or concerns.

1. _____

2. _____

3. _____

4. _____

5. _____

6. _____

Control Check

It is a good idea to divide your personal worries into two categories. (Those worries over which you feel you have control and those worries which you probably can't change no matter how hard you try.)

List your personal worries again, but this time write the worries that you feel you **can** control on the front burners of the stovetop on the next page. Next list your personal worries that you feel you **cannot** control on the back burners of the stovetop.

Look at the following example of how this might be done.

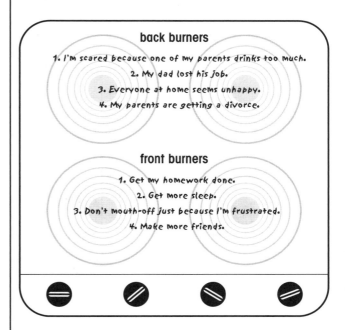

back burners
1. I'm scared because one of my parents drinks too much.
2. My dad lost his job.
3. Everyone at home seems unhappy.
4. My parents are getting a divorce.

front burners
1. Get my homework done.
2. Get more sleep.
3. Don't mouth-off just because I'm frustrated.
4. Make more friends.

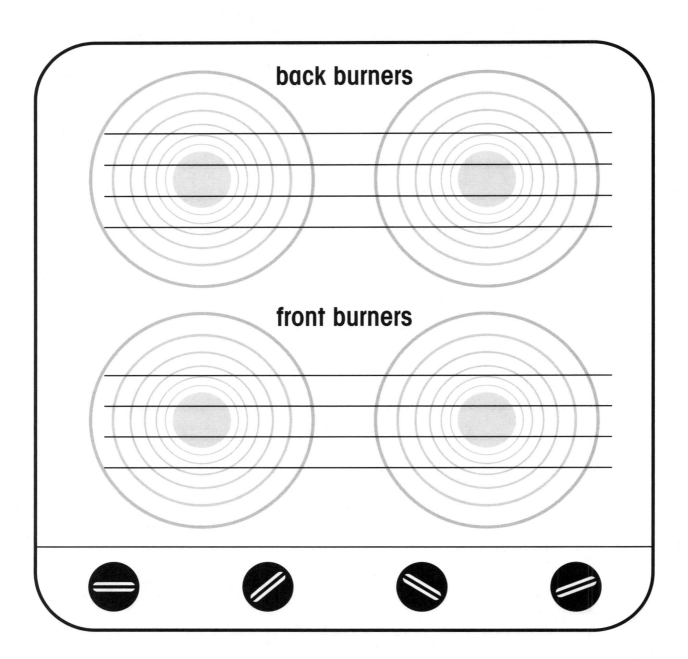

back burners

front burners

The worries that you listed on the back burners don't mean that you don't care or don't want things to change. It just means that these worries are situations that at this time in your life will probably be there for a long time; and if they are taken off of the stove as a result of time or other circumstances, it probably won't be as a result of your actions.

The worries that you listed on the front burners are concerns that you can probably change with effort. These are concerns on which you should focus your energy.

Ask yourself the following questions:

1. What is it that you really want to change?

_____

_____

2. Who are the people I trust that can encourage me to change what I can?

_____

_____

3. What are at least three (3) specific things you can start to do to get or accomplish what you really want?

1. _____

_____

2. _____

_____

3. _____

_____

These steps are good things to talk over with a trusted adult such as a parent, teacher, or counselor. While you have the ability to work out problems in your life, it is good to connect with adults you trust to review your plan.

Good luck and stay focused on what you can control.

Reprinted with permission from Frank, K. and Smith-Rex, S., (1996), *Getting Over the Blues: A Kid's Guide to Understanding and Coping with Unpleasant Feelings and Depression.* Minneapolis, MN: Educational Media.

Strategy 16:
Biofeedback

(suggested grade levels 5-12)

Stress Cards

Stress cards read our stress level through our body's feedback. When a person feels anxious, upset, angry, or some other strong emotion, his/her blood is drawn inward causing cold hands. If a person is greatly stressed, the card will register black. When a person is calm, the card will show a blue color. The stress card works best at normal room temperature. On the back of the card are four ideas for reducing stress. This stress card can offer regular feedback to manage your stress and anger level (Bowman, R., 2001). Stress cards may be ordered through Youthlight, Inc. at (800) 209-9774.

Stress Mapping

This exercise can be done by simply drawing a silhouette of a body. Now think carefully about where you usually feel stress and shade those parts of the body in the drawing. Some people, for example, feel stress in their shoulders, hands, chest, stomach, head, etc.

Once you recognize where you wear your stress, you can do something about it. For example, if you become aware of stress in a certain area of your body, this is your body's way of telling you to back off and relax. Our bodies are designed to let us know when they are stressed. It is important for us to listen to what our bodies are telling us.

Make Believe

Imagine or visualize yourself in a situation that would normally create anxiety. Now picture yourself handling this situation in a good way. Notice the positive thoughts you give yourself. Also, notice what you do and say that helps you to feel in control. On a regular basis, practice handling challenging situations by using this technique in advance.

Strategy 17:
Refocusing
(suggested grade levels 5-12)

Most of the things about which people worry never happen. This is why when negative or bad thoughts cross our minds, we need to **refocus** or change our thinking. You have a choice to worry or to think about something good. How are you going to use your time and energy? **Refocus** simply means to focus again on what you need to do and to think positively. Take charge of your thinking. Get rid of negative thoughts, and put in positive thoughts.

Strategy 18:
False Alarm Disconnect
(suggested grade levels 4-12)

How the brain works is important to understand. The brain naturally alerts us to danger such as a fast approaching storm or a nearby poisonous snake. The brain does its job well to protect us. However, with some people, the brain can sound a false alarm. This usually has to do with the chemicals in the brain getting out of balance. When this happens, people worry or fear things that are not really dangerous. One example is someone being afraid to go to school even though he or she can't point to any real problem. Another example is when a child is unable to sleep in his or her own room even though the home is safe and secure.

When this type of fear and anxiety starts, it is necessary to turn off the alarm. You can do this by telling yourself that this is only a "false alarm," and that it is OK. By continuing to give yourself "clear messages" or positive thoughts, the false alarms are normally disconnected. If, however, this doesn't work in spite of your best efforts, certain medications can often help. Your doctor can prescribe medications, if necessary, that will also help you to turn off those false alarms. Counseling can help with this, too.

Strategy 19:
Reducing FAT
(suggested grade levels 5-12)

While our feelings are a very special and important part of us, they can cause us big problems if we don't manage them well. Just imagine if you let anger control your life, how many people would avoid you. Imagine if you let fear run your life, how it would trap you from going places and doing normal things.

Here's how feelings get us in trouble. It's called **FAT.**

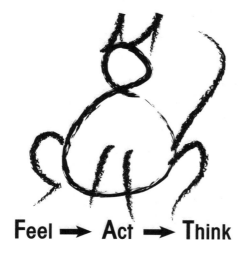

Feel ➔ Act ➔ Think

Let's say a person feels worried about catching germs. Without thinking through it, this person acts afraid to go anywhere and constantly washes his hands. By this point, the feelings of worry are so strong that thinking clearly is hard to do. Our feelings have taken over.

Now let's go to a **low fat thinking diet.** In order to do this, we only need to rearrange two letters.

F A T ➔ F T A
Feel ➔ Act ➔ Think   Feel ➔ Think ➔ Act

Now watch what happens. When the person feels worry about germs, his brain takes over. He thinks, "I know germs are out there, but I'm just going to be doing normal stuff. As long as I remember to wash my hands before I eat, I'll be O.K." With this clear thinking, the person goes on and has a good time.

Remember

F eel ....Noticing that your feelings are normal

T hink ....Thinking clearly through the situation

A ct ....Acting wisely

More Tips For Facing Common Fears

The strategies presented to this point are general in nature. They can be used to help deal with all types of anxiety in all kinds of situations. The following strategies, however, are for specific types of anxiety. Each common fear that kids often face has at least two strategies to overcome the problem.

1. Sleeping Alone in My Room

Try this: *Sleeping Bag Shuffle*

If you are sleeping in your parents' room, it's time to start moving to your room. It's more fun there anyway since all your "stuff" is in there. At bedtime grab your sleeping bag. Pick a spot to sleep that is at least a little closer to your room. Each night or two, pick a new spot closer and closer to your room. Before you know it, you'll be shuffling back to your own room and your own bed.

Try this: *Instant Companion*

Have a pet stay in your room. A dog, cat, hamster, guinea pig, etc. can be a best friend at bedtime. These pets can give us a feeling of being safe and can get our minds on something good. Also, see "Magic Number" under common fear number five (page 74), Being Alone and Away from Trusted Adults. This plan works well to help you discover that all is well.

2. Being Afraid of the Dark

Try this: *The Light Dimmer*

Have your parent(s) get a light dimmer switch for you. A dimming night-light is best. Every night dim it a little more. Before long, you won't be afraid of the dark.

Try this: *Come to Your Senses*

When it's dark, you can use your four other senses to feel safe and secure. Think of how blind people bravely face life every day. They especially use their senses of hearing and touch. While in bed, listen to sounds around you. You'll probably hear your family moving about. This tells you all is O.K. Perhaps you would want to listen to your radio or a CD. Also, hold a special object such as a special blanket or stuffed animal.

Try this: *Camp Out*

Pretend you are camping in your room. A good camper will always have a flashlight. Just turn on your flashlight anytime you feel afraid, and you'll see that all is well.

3. Monsters and Scary Things

Try this: *Monster Spray and Flashlight*

Have your parent get a "Monster Spray Bottle" for you. Spray it all around your room just before bedtime. Use a flashlight from time to time, and you'll see that the monsters are gone.

Try this: *Go Figure*

Draw or write out a safety plan. Kids often have the best ideas to overcome fears. By coming up with some ideas such as leaving on a night-light, arranging stuffed animals around the bed, or sleeping with a special blanket, you'll have sweet dreams.

Try this: *Draw a Picture*

By drawing a picture of the "monster" and discussing it with a trusted adult, you will see that the "monster" isn't so bad. After all, think about it. That monster has never hurt you. You are safe and sound!

Try this: *It's All in the Mind*

Remind yourself that monsters are only imaginary. Instead think about a fun activity you like to do or a place you like to go. Good thoughts bring good dreams.

4. Worry About Too Much To Do

Try this: *Secret Code Word WIN*

WIN stands for **W**hat's **I**mportant **N**ow (Holtz, 1998). Make a list of all the things you need to do. Now, circle the ones that are most urgent and important. Do these first and you will **WIN**.

Try this: *Make a Worry List*

List all your worries. Now put them into two categories. Category One includes the ones over which you have no control. Realize that most things people worry about never happen. In Category Two, list the worries you can do something about. Prioritize this second list. The ones at the bottom of your "control list" will just have to wait. Take care of the big things in your life first.

5. Being Alone and Away from Trusted Adults

Try this: *"Magic Number"*

Practice going places for short periods of time away from others. For example, go up to your room by yourself. Choose a "magic number" such as one or two minutes. Using a watch or timer, stay away by yourself for the time chosen. An adult can check on you each time the magic number is up. Repeat this over and over. This magic number should increase to three, four, five, even ten or more minutes as the days go on. After awhile, it will be like magic as you go places without being afraid.

Try this: *Get a Life*

When faced with being away from your close friends or family, be sure to have a plan. Have an activity to do that helps you pass the time. What is it that you love to do? Distract yourself with a good computer game, T.V. program, sporting activity, music, or art. What is your fancy?

6. Being Afraid of School

Try this: *School Mapping*

Draw a map from where you get dropped off at school to your homeroom. Make a plan to walk in by yourself to various points on your school map. For example, walk to the door by yourself before getting the counselor or someone to help you further. Day by day, go a little further into the building by yourself as planned and mark your progress on the school map. Eventually, you will be able to walk into school and have a good day.

Try this: *Focus on Your Friends*

One of the greatest things about school is developing friendships. Kids that have trouble going to school usually miss their friends the most. Call a friend or two and plan to meet them at school. Let these friends be a part of your support system. Have some fun and school will start to feel better.

Try this: *Partial Schedule*

If you don't think you can make it through the whole day, think about going part of the school day. A doctor, therapist, and school counselor can work out a program that fits your situation. The goal is to start with a schedule that gives you confidence, even if it is for just a few minutes or one class. Gradually increase the time spent at school. Once you get some momentum going, you'll be surprised how quickly you can get back to a normal schedule. Be sure to keep up with your schoolwork when on a partial schedule. Your doctor may need to request homebound instruction until you get back to normal.

7. Test Anxiety

Try this: *Learn the Secret Code Word **IOTA**.*

IOTA stands for **It**'s **O**nly a **T**est **A**nyway. Study hard, think good thoughts, and just do your best.

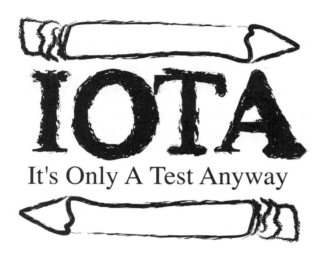

It's Only A Test Anyway

Try this: *Be a Test-Buster*

Dr. Robert Bowman at the University of South Carolina has done a lot of work on test anxiety. It's normal to feel nervous before a test, but too much worry will keep you from thinking clearly. Dr. Bowman suggests the following four tips in order to be a Test-Buster (1987):

a. Prepare for the Test

Before a big test, eat a good breakfast, get lots of sleep, and, of course, study.

b. Know How to Get Rid of the Test Monster

Put it into perspective. It's only a test, so just do your best. Talk to yourself about it in a good way (see page 58). Use relaxation and deep breathing techniques (see pages 48-49). Also, the *Chill Out Plan* on page 52 may be of help. Ridding your mind and body of stress will improve your chances of doing well.

c. Getting Motivated to Do Your Best

Get focused on the test only. You've no doubt studied hard, and you are smart. Bring out your tenacity (that means giving it all you've got.) Just as you would do your best in a sporting event, dare to do your very best on the test. That's all you can do. You'll then be proud of yourself. You may not get the highest score, but you will feel satisfied that you gave an honest effort. No one is good at everything, but everyone is good at something. Find your strengths and build on them. If taking tests is not your thing, just do your best. You'll get better and better as you relax and give it your best shot.

d. Become Test-Wise.
Learn Test-Taking Tips

Here are a few examples:

1) On a multiple-choice test, eliminate the obvious wrong answers first. Then look carefully at the remaining choices. Usually the correct choice will become clear. If not, go with your hunch. The answer that seems correct usually is correct.

2) If you get stuck on a question or problem, skip it for the time being and move on to the next one. Later go back and tackle the one you skipped. Often after giving it some time, the problem or question will become more clear and easier to answer.

3) Always go back at the end of the test and check for careless mistakes such as spelling, grammar, and punctuation. In math, look for computation errors or misplaced decimal points. Make sure all questions have been answered.

4) Preview the test. Briefly look over the whole test. As you read the questions, jot down brief notes that you may use later as you answer all the questions. Plan to answer the easy questions first and the most difficult ones last.

5) When taking essay tests, think before you write. Briefly outline your answers. Quickly write down ideas you want to include while answering each question.

6) On essay tests, use the first paragraph as an overview of your essay. Use the following paragraphs to discuss these main points in detail.

A couple of good books among many others in which to find more study and test-taking tips are the following: *Study Power: Study Skills to Improve Your Learning and Your Grades,* by Wood Smethurst and William R. Luckie, Ph.D., (Brookline Books) and *How to Do Your Best on Tests* by Sara Dulaney Gilbert (Beech Tree Books).

8. Fear of School Bullies

Try this: *Don't Go It Alone*

Talk to trusted adults such as your teacher or counselor. You are not expected to handle bullies alone. It is the school's job to make sure every student feels safe. School officials can then take care of the problem.

Try this: *Make Friends and Believe in Yourself*

So you are not an easy target for others to bully, try to develop some good friendships and go with a good group whenever possible. Also, keep your head up, look others in the eye, and show confidence. When you look in control, others are less likely to bother you.

9. Fear of Germs and Getting Sick

Try this: *Divide and Conquer*

Think of places and things where you feel afraid of catching germs. The fact is that most places are usually safe and most things won't cause you to get sick such as going to the store, riding on the bus, touching dirt, etc. The odds are greatly in your favor. To quit going places and doing normal things will only trap you. So, if you are afraid let's say to go to parties and other get-togethers with large groups because you are afraid of catching an illness, start small by going to a friend's house. Later involve two or three friends doing a short activity. Gradually work up to doing more and more things in larger settings. The key is to gradually try to do more and more. Slowly but surely move out of your comfort zone.

Try this: *Time It*

If you're in a habit of constantly washing your hands, make yourself resist the temptation for a period of time. Gradually increase the time periods from minutes to hours. Likewise, if you are afraid to go to certain places, make yourself go and stay for a designated period of time. Keep doing this over and over for longer time periods.

10. Fear of Terrorism

Try this: *Gather, Gab, and Go On*

Get the facts on current events. Talk it over with trusted adults and friends. Sharing feelings and thoughts always helps. Finally, focus on moving on with life. There are so many good places to go and things to do. Refocus your energy on normal things.

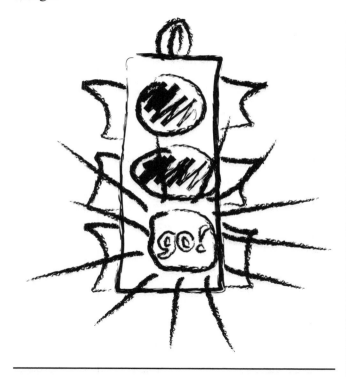

Try this:: *Consider the Odds*

The odds of being involved in a terrorist attack are very low. Use your clear mind and go on with life as normally as possible.

11. Social Anxiety

Try this: *Friendship Model*

Use the following four steps to break through into a few good friendships. Having a friend or two can help you to face social situations and activities.

a. Check It Out

Look for people who send clear messages. There are always people who appear kind and open to a friendship. Look for the people with warm smiles and caring attitudes. Also, look for someone who has something in common with you.

b. Reach Out

Whether or not you are shy, go up to the person with clear messages and strike up a conversation. Do this by simply asking a question or giving a compliment.

c. Try It Out

Give it some time and you'll see if this friendship is meant to be. If it is not working, check it out again and look for another friendship. More often than not, when you use these steps, friendships start to happen.

d. Work It Out

Keep the friendship going. Work at the friendship. Give and take. Be a friend!

Try this: *Do Little Things That Add Up*

Social anxiety has a lot to do with worry about what others think. When we feel that others are judging us, we naturally feel nervous. A person with social anxiety is overly nervous. A good way to combat this is to build your confidence. Start doing things that you know you can do. Gradually stretch yourself to do more and more in social situations whether it's saying hello to someone, telling a joke, or even giving a short speech at school.

12. Fear of Animals

Try this: *Desensitize Yourself*

The key here is to face your fears gradually. Over a period of time, go with a trusted adult and move closer and closer to animals that you know are safe such as a friendly neighborhood dog. Eventually pet the animal and become more and more playful. You decide how much more you can do each step of the way. Stretch yourself out of your comfort zone little by little.

Try this: *The Healing Species*

Talk to your teacher or school counselor about having "The Healing Species" come to your school. They teach children how to care for animals and bring dogs that have been abused into the classroom to teach kids compassion. Contact YouthLight, Inc. for more information about this program.

Try this: *Animal Zone*

Have a designated enclosed place to house a safe animal. Visit the animal from closer and closer distances. Stay nearby longer and longer. Eventually, the animal will become a friend.

13. Fear of Small or Tight Places (Claustrophobia)

Try this: *Scavenger Hunt*

Go on a scavenger hunt where prizes are located in cramped or small areas. The visits to each area should be brief. Continue to do more scavenger hunts over many weeks with longer visits required at each spot to get the prize.

Try this: *Personal Coaching*

Go with a "coach." Bring a friend or trusted adult who can "coach" and coax you through tight places. You're not alone and can be constantly encouraged.

14. Fear of Loss or Abandonment

Try this: *Keeping Track*

Write down on a sheet of paper or mark a clock as to when your parent or loved one will return from work or wherever he or she goes. Notice that your parent or loved one will return on time as promised. Eventually, you'll see that there is no need to worry.

Try this: *They Have to Come Back*

Have your parent or loved one give you something they own which they'll have to come back and get. For example, your parent may give you a favorite book or picture that he or she wouldn't want to lose. They'll always return to claim this item, so take good care of it.

15. Fear of Failure

Try this: *Don't Worry. Be Happy.*

Accept the fact that everyone makes mistakes and fails. In fact, when we fail, we often can learn the most. We figure out what we need to do to succeed next time. Remember, Babe Ruth struck out a lot more than he hit homeruns. Nevertheless, he is still considered by many to be the best baseball player ever. So relax and do your best. Have a positive attitude!

Try this: *Record Your Successes*

Write down your milestones. When you accomplish something significant, record it in your journal. Whether it is getting an A on a test, winning a race, or doing a recital at school, they all count. You'll see that your successes add up and far outweigh your failures.

A Few Final Words

You have read and pondered several activities and ideas now that I trust will be helpful to you in your situation. You probably cannot do them all. It is my hope that you'll find the ones that especially fit you best and put them to good use. Good effort on your part in using these techniques makes all the difference. Just do your best, and I trust good things will happen. If you have any thoughts about the ideas and techniques in this book, I would welcome them. Please pass them along to Youthlight, Inc. Best wishes and may you have great success!

References

American Psychiatric Association. (1994). *Diagnostic and statistical manual of mental disorders (4th ed.).* Washington, DC: Author.

Bowman, R. (1987). *Test buster pep rally.* Minneapolis, MN: Educational Media.

Bowman & Bowman. (1997). *Chill out bag.* Chapin, SC: Youthlight.

Davis, J. (2000). Childhood anxiety steadily on the rise since the 1950s. *MyWebMD.* Retrieved June 26, 2002, from http://my.webmd.com/content/article/1728.66815.

Frank, K., & Smith-Rex, S. (1996). *Getting over the blues: A kid's guide to understanding and coping with unpleasant feelings and depression.* Minneapolis, MN: Educational Media.

Goldman, W. T. (2001, June 28). Childhood and adolescent anxiety disorders. *Keepkidshealthy.com.* Retrieved June 26, 2002, from http://www.keepkidshealthy.com/welcome/conditions/anxiety_disorders.html.

Gorman, C. (2002, June 10). The science of anxiety. *Time*, pp. 46-54.

Holtz, L. (1998). *Winning every day: The game plan for success.* New York, NY: HarperBusiness.

Manassis, K. (1996). *Keys to parenting your anxious child.* Retrieved July 27, 2002, from http://www.amazon.com/exec/obidos/-ASIN/0812096053.

National Alliance for the Mentally Ill. (2001). *NAMI helpline fact sheet.* Retrieved June 27, 2002, from http://www.nami.org/helpline/-anxiety.htm.

National Institute of Mental Health. (2001, April 26). *Medication effective in treating anxiety disorders in children and adolescents.* Retrieved June 25, 2002, from http://www.nimh.nih.gov/events/prrupp.cfm.

Park, A. (2002, June 10). The anatomy of anxiety. *Time.* pp. 50-51.

Rapee, R. M. (Ed.). Spence, S., Cobham, V., & Wignall, A. (2000). *Helping your anxious child: A step-by-step guide for parents.* Retrieved July 27, 2002, from http://www.amazon.com/exec/obidos/ASIN/1572241918.

Wilens, T. E. (1999). *Straight talk about psychiatric medications for kids.* New York: Guilford.